The Young Geographer Investigates

Temperate Forests

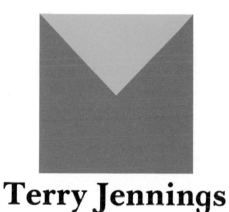

Terry Jennings

Oxford University Press

Oxford University Press, Walton Street, Oxford OX2 6DP

Oxford New York Toronto
Delhi Bombay Calcutta Madras Karachi
Kuala Lumpur Singapore Hong Kong Tokyo
Nairobi Dar es Salaam Cape Town
Melbourne Auckland Madrid

and associated companies in
Berlin Ibadan

Oxford is a trade mark of Oxford University Press

Oxford University Press 1986

ISBN 0 19 917076 2 (Paperback)
First published 1986
Reprinted 1989, 1991, 1993

ISBN 0 19 917082 7 (Hardback)
First published 1986
Reprinted 1990, 1991

© Terry Jennings 1986

Typeset in Great Britain by
Tradespools Limited, Frome, Somerset
Printed in Hong Kong

Acknowledgements

The publishers thank the following for permission to reproduce transparencies:

B & C Alexander p.26 (bottom right); Heather Angel p.35 (left);
Ardea p.10, p.11 (left); Aspect Picture Library p.37 (top right);
A-Z Botanical Collection Ltd. p.41; Janet and Colin Bord p.39 (bottom right);
The Bridgeman Art Library p.27 (bottom left); J. Allan Cash p.32 (bottom right);
Bruce Coleman Ltd./Hans Reinhard p.12 (top); Coleman/Frith p.32 (inset);
Bruce Coleman Ltd. p.37 (left); Coleman/Halle Flygare p.39 (top right);
Forestry Commission p.9 (left), p.14 (bottom), p.16 (centre left, centre right),
p.17 (right), p.18 (top right), p.26 (bottom left);
Susan Griggs/Horst Munzig p.13 (left); Griggs/Victor Englebert p.14 (top);
Griggs/Adam Woolfitt p.26 (top right); Griggs/Mike Warman p.30 (bottom
left); Robert Harding Picture Library p.15 (top and bottom), p.34 (top right);
Harding/Walter Rawlings p.18 (left); Harding/Jon Gardey p.38 (inset left);
Chris Honeywell/OUP © p.29 (top left), p.42;
Jacana Scientific Control p.12 (bottom); Terry Jennings p.7 (top and right), p.11
(top and right), p.13 (inset and bottom right), p.16 (bottom left), p.17 (top left),
p.25, p.29 (bottom left), p.30 (top left), p.33 (right);
Frank Lane Agency/Steve McCutcheon p.34 (left);
Lane/Irene Vandermolen p.34 (bottom right); Long Ashton Research Station
p.30 (inset and bottom right); Mansell Collection p.31;
Midland Veneers p.27 (top left and right); Oxford Scientific Films/G.I. Bernard
p.6 (left and right), p.7 (left); Portuguese Government Trade Office p.32
(top right); Rapho p.13 (top right); Bernard Regent p.26 (top left); Rentokill
p.46 (left and right); Rothamsted Experimental Station p.39 (bottom left);
Spectrum Colour Library p.9 (right), p.16 (top left), p.17 (bottom left),
p.32 (left); Tony Stone Associates cover; Survival Anglia/Alan Root
p.18 (bottom right); Survival Anglia p.35 (right); Survival Anglia/Jeff Foott
p.37 (bottom right); Jenny Thomas p.33 (left); John Topham Picture Library
p.9 (top), p.15 (left), p.36, p.38 (top and bottom)

Illustrations by Norma Burgin Steve Cocking Roger Gorringe Peter Joyce
Ed McLachlan Ben Manchipp David More Nick Mynheer John Pearson
Mike Saunders Tudor Artists Michael Whittlesea

Contents

The temperate regions of the world 4
The parts of a tree 5
How a tree makes its food 6
Death and decay 7
A world of forests 8
Coniferous trees 9
Deciduous trees 10
The seasons in a deciduous forest 11
Deer and bison 12
Using trees 13
Felling trees 14
Transporting felled trees 15
New forests from old 16
Planting a forest plantation 17
Fire 18
Do you remember? 19
Things to do 20
Things to find out 25
Wood 26
Other kinds of wood 27
Paper 28
Charcoal 29
Apple orchards 30
The hunting forests of Europe 31
The forests of the Mediterranean region 32
The northern coniferous forests 33
People in the northern coniferous forests 34
The tallest and oldest trees in the world 35
China and Japan 36
Australian eucalyptus forests 37
Forests for leisure 38
The forests return 39
Do you remember? 40
Things to do 41
Things to find out 46
Glossary 47
Index 48

The temperate regions of the world

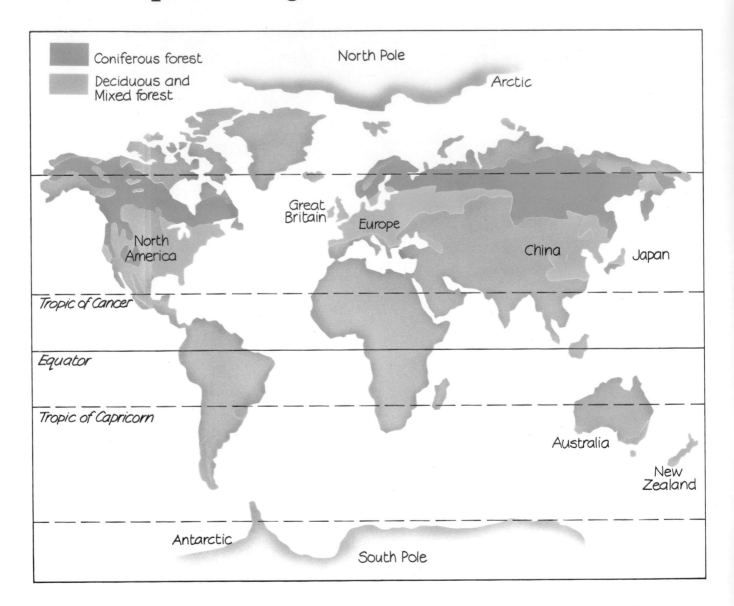

Coniferous forest

Deciduous and Mixed forest

North Pole

Arctic

Great Britain

Europe

North America

China

Japan

Tropic of Cancer

Equator

Tropic of Capricorn

Australia

New Zealand

Antarctic

South Pole

This book is about the forests which occur in the temperate regions of the world. These are the parts of the world between the tropics and the polar regions.

In the tropics, near the Equator, the days are long and hot. There are no big differences between the seasons.

As you move away from the tropics, towards the Poles, the summers are still warm, although they are shorter. And the winters are longer and cooler. These are the temperate regions of the world. Within the temperate regions the climate varies a lot. In fact the temperate regions have all kinds of weather. But where there is enough rain, and the summers are not too short, forests can grow.

Near the North and South Poles, it is cold throughout the year. The summers are very short. The winters are long, dark and bitterly cold. It is too cold and the summers are too short for trees to grow.

4

The parts of a tree

Trees are large, woody plants. They are the world's largest plants. All trees have three main parts. There is a thick woody stem called a trunk. Then there is the crown of the tree, made up of leaves and branches. The very thin branches are called twigs. At certain times of the year there may be buds, flowers or fruit on the twigs.

At the base of the tree are a large number of spreading roots. Some trees have one large root called a tap root. The tap root grows deep into the soil. It has smaller roots growing from it. Other trees have many large and small roots. The roots often spread as far underground as the twigs spread in the crown of the tree.

The roots anchor the tree. They stop strong winds blowing the tree over. Roots also take up huge amounts of water from the soil. In one day the roots of a large oak tree may take up well over 200 litres of water from the soil.

crown
leaves
branch
twig
tap root
trunk
root

How a tree makes its food

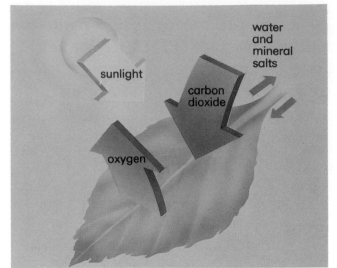

The leaves make food for the tree. The green substance in leaves is called chlorophyll. To make food, the leaves use the water and mineral salts that the roots take up from the soil. The water and mineral salts travel up the tree to little tubes in the veins of the leaves. The leaves also need sunshine and a gas from the air called carbon dioxide to make their food. The green chlorophyll in the leaves uses the sunshine to turn the water, carbon dioxide and mineral salts into food. One of the waste products of this process is oxygen. Most trees do not grow well in shady places, because there is not enough sunlight for the leaves to make their food properly.

Many trees lose all their leaves in winter. These are called deciduous trees. Oak, ash, elm, sycamore and beech are common deciduous trees. Deciduous trees grow new leaves in the spring.

Some trees keep their leaves in the winter. These are called evergreen trees. Holly, pine, yew and laurel are a few evergreen trees. The leaves of evergreen trees do not last for ever. They fall off a few at a time all through the year.

Deciduous tree in summer

Deciduous tree in winter

6

Death and decay

Oak leaves

When leaves fall from a tree, they lie in the wind and rain on the ground. Gradually they rot or decay into the soil. Animals such as woodlice, earthworms and millipedes also eat pieces off the dead leaves. Tiny plants such as bacteria and fungi also break up the materials that make up the leaves. Slowly, the leaves are changed to mineral salts in the soil. The mineral salts can then be used as food by other plants. The dead leaves act as natural fertilizers for the living plants. All kinds of plants, including trees, use the mineral salts from the dead leaves to help them grow.

When other parts of the tree fall, including the trunk, branches and twigs, they too decay away. They also form mineral salts which other plants can use as food. In the cooler parts of the world decay takes place slowly. In woodlands and forests in the cooler parts of the world there is often a thick layer of leaves and twigs on the ground. The leaves and twigs of evergreen trees decay very slowly.

A decayed holly leaf

A felled oak tree being fed on by bracket fungi

A world of forests

Once, long ago, much of Europe and North America was covered in forests. The mountain slopes were covered with evergreen forests of fir, spruce and pine trees. So were the northern parts of these continents. Most of the rest of the land was covered with deciduous forests. Herds of deer and bison roamed through the forests. Wolves, lynxes and bears hunted there.

The first people lived in caves. They ate whatever they could find or catch, and travelled long distances to hunt food. Later, people learned how to use fire. They used fire to keep themselves warm. Fire could also change the taste of meat and plants. The people had learned to cook. Before long people discovered how to plant seeds and grow crops for their meals. They used fire to make clearings in the forest to plant their crops. There was no longer any need to go a long way to look for food. The people could stay longer in one place and build a hut to live in.

As the number of people increased, so more and more of the forest was cleared. Eventually there were large towns and cities. There were farms, roads, schools, shops and factories. Most of these were on land which had once been covered by forests.

Many cities in temperate Europe are built where ancient forests grew. Here is London in medieval times

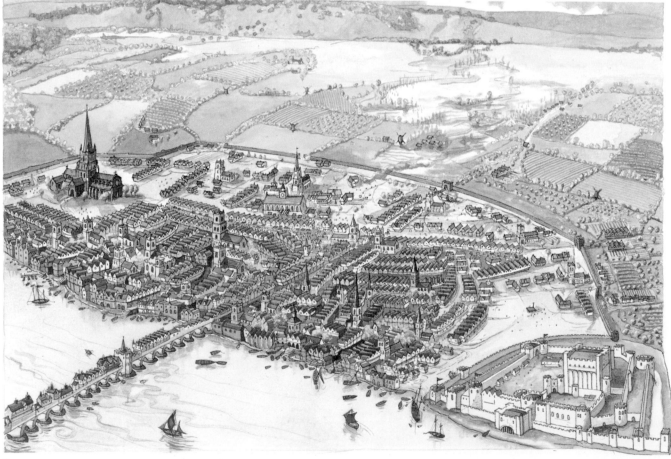

Coniferous trees

Some trees lose their leaves in winter. These are deciduous trees. The trees which remain green all the year round are called evergreens.

In the temperate regions of the world, most of the evergreen trees have their seeds in cones. These are called coniferous trees, or conifers. Pine, spruce and fir are some coniferous trees. Coniferous trees have narrow, needle-shaped leaves. These little leaves help the tree to save water. The branches on conifers also slant downwards so that heavy snow slides off.

particularly well where the soil is poor. There are many kinds of conifers. They include the world's largest and the world's oldest living things. Conifers also form the world's largest forests.

Conifers can grow in much colder places than deciduous trees. They are found near to the polar regions. The line beyond which trees cannot grow on a mountain is called the tree-line. Conifers can grow right up to the tree-line on mountains. But conifers are also found in the warmer, drier parts of the world. They grow

You can see the tree-line on this mountain in Canada

9

Deciduous trees

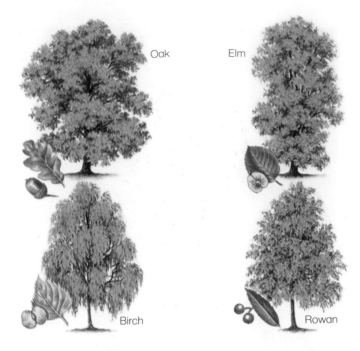

Some caterpillars feed on forest oak trees

Deciduous forests grow nearer to the Equator than the big northern coniferous forests. Deciduous forests grow in places where the summers are warm and the winters are not too cold. They contain trees like oak, ash, elm, sycamore and birch.

The branches of deciduous trees spread out widely to catch the sun.

Their leaves are a brighter green than the leaves or needles of conifers. The water in the leaves makes them soft and juicy. They are eaten by many insects and other creatures.

Deciduous trees grow in the most fertile areas of temperate regions. Many of the deciduous forests have been cleared to make way for farmland and cities. At one time deciduous forests covered large areas of Europe and North America. Now only patches of the original forests remain.

Layers of growth in a deciduous forest
Insets: purple emperor butterfly, grey squirrel, fly agaric mushroom, and millipede

The seasons in a deciduous forest

Inside an evergreen forest, one season is very much like another. But in a deciduous forest there are big differences between the seasons. During the winter the trees are bare. A thick carpet of dead leaves covers the floor of the forest. When the weather is cold, only a few animals come out. Some, such as hedgehogs, dormice, chipmunks and black bears are hibernating. Hibernating means sleeping through the winter months.

A sea of spring bluebells

A dormouse hibernating

During the spring the weather gets better and the temperatures begin to rise. Most of the smaller plants start to flower. They grow, bloom and produce their seeds before the trees above them have opened their leaves and cut off the light. As the tree leaves open, many insects hatch out on the branches. They feed on the tender young tree leaves. Thousands of birds arrive after spending the winter further south. They breed, and feed their young on the millions of insects. Larger animals such as deer also feed on the tree leaves. Many more birds and animals feed on the fruits, nuts and seeds produced by the trees.

Autumn leaves

As autumn approaches, the days are shorter and colder. The trees can no longer obtain enough water from the soil. The leaves die and turn yellow, orange, red or brown. When the leaves fall, they form food for fungi and small animals in the soil.

11

Deer and bison

Red deer

In many temperate forests, deer are the largest animals to be found. The most common kind of deer in the northern forests is the red deer. In North America red deer are called wapiti. Red deer are also found in the forests of New Zealand, where they were taken by early settlers. Red deer feed on tree leaves. They also eat the grass which grows in the clearings.

Male red deer are called stags, the females hinds. In the autumn, the largest stags try to take control of a group of hinds. They may fight and drive off the weaker stags. After they have mated with the hinds, the strong stags leave. The young, or calves, are born in the early summer.

In some parts of the north, the enemies of red deer are wolves, lynx and bears. Where there are none of these animals, the red deer have to be controlled by people hunting with rifles. If this was not done, there would soon be too many deer and they would damage the forest.

Another large animal which feeds on tree leaves is the European bison. Once millions of bison lived all over eastern and central Europe. They almost became extinct in the wild in the 1920s because too many were hunted and shot. Fortunately there were still some left in zoos and parks. Now the only remaining wild herds of bison roam in the forests on the Russian-Polish border. They are protected by law.

Bison

Using trees

Wood is one of our most valuable materials. People have always used wood. Even Stone Age people used wood for arrows, clubs and the handles of stone tools. Wood was also used as a fuel.

Today wood is still an important fuel in many parts of the world. It is also used for buildings, fences and bridges. The walls of some houses are made from wood. But all houses have a lot of wood inside them. A great deal of wood goes into house roofs. More is used in floors, doors and ceilings. Most furniture contains at least some wood. Many musical instruments have wood in them. A lot of toys and tools have wood in them. Some sports equipment is made from wood.

charcoal and turpentine come from such trees. Some of our foods also come from trees. They include apples, pears, peaches, plums, chestnuts, hazel-nuts, walnuts and almonds. From wood, wood pulp is made. This is used to make paper and artificial silk or rayon.

Picking walnuts in France

We use huge amounts of wood. Some of it comes from natural forests. But nowadays much of it comes from plantations. These are forests that are specially planted and managed by people.

Cuckoo clocks are usually made of wood

We also use a number of other materials made from trees which grow in temperate forests. Cork,

A tree plantation

Felling trees

Felling with an axe

Speedy felling with a chain-saw

Until 30 or 40 years ago, most forest trees were cut down or felled by hand. People used axes and long saws to cut through the tree trunk. Great care was needed to see that the tree fell in the right direction. First a V-shaped cut was made on the side facing the way the tree was to fall. Another cut was then made a little higher up on the other side of the tree. Then the tree would fall under its own weight. More recently powerful chain-saws have been used to fell trees. To cut a tree with a chain-saw is not such hard work as using a hand saw. But the same skill and care is needed to see that the tree falls safely.

In the last 10 years or so, many other machines have come along to help the forester. These machines are particularly useful in forest plantations.

14

Some of the machines can go up to a large tree and fell it. At the same time they slice off the top and all the branches. Then the most valuable part, the trunk, is loaded straight on to a lorry. Other machines pick up the branches and smaller pieces of timber. They grind these up into small chips from which paper can be made. In this way, nothing is wasted.

A 'tree-hugger' cuts and carries logs

Transporting felled trees

The felled trees are taken to the sawmills and pulpmills. In most forests, the tree trunks are dragged out of the forest along specially made tracks. Powerful tractors are often used for this. In some forests a system of special pulleys, like a crane, drags the felled trees out of the forest. The trunks are usually taken to the sawmills by road. Special lorries are used.

Log sorting by river in Canada

A tractor hauling logs

In the past, much timber was taken to the sawmills by river. The logs were floated down the river. But rivers are used very little nowadays. Partly this is because lorries have become cheaper, but also because logs were often lost in the rivers. And the work was dangerous with many workers being killed or injured.

Another problem with river transport is that the pulp mills need timber all the year round. In winter, however, the rivers are often frozen so that the timber cannot be moved. Helicopters and hovercraft are sometimes used to carry felled trees. But these are very expensive to use.

Transportation by helicopter

15

New forests from old

A tree nursery

Large numbers of tree seeds fall to the ground around the parent tree. Some of these seeds grow and produce new trees. This is the way a natural forest grows and spreads.

Some kinds of deciduous trees can grow again from the cut stumps. The young trunks may be cut back every few years. In this way, large numbers of thin sticks are produced. This is known as coppicing. Much coppiced wood is still used for firewood, for fences, brushes and for thatching roofs.

Coppiced woodland in Cambridgeshire

Nowadays many trees are grown in plantations. These trees grow from seeds planted by the foresters who are the people that manage the forest. Sometimes the seeds are collected from the ground. More often they are picked from the trees. To do this the forester may climb up a net. Or he or she may use a 'tree bicycle' to help climb the tree.

Two methods of collecting seeds

If the seeds were planted straight in a forest, most would be eaten by birds and animals. And any seedlings which did grow would soon be choked by weeds. Instead the seeds are sown in a tree nursery. They are sown in long narrow beds. There the seeds can be weeded and protected. When the seedlings are big enough they are taken from the seed beds. They are planted out in rows where they have more room to grow. After another year or two, the young trees are ready to be planted in the forest.

Planting a forest plantation

A hillside ploughed ready for young trees

Before a new forest can be planted, the land has to be made ready. If it is open ground it can be ploughed. But old woodland has first of all to be cleared. The old tree stumps are often pushed into long ridges which shelter the young trees. The land is then fenced. This keeps out people and also animals which might eat the young trees.

Tree planting on a hillside

Young and mature trees side by side in a plantation

The young trees are usually planted during the autumn, winter or early spring. At these times the young trees are resting. Young trees are usually planted 1.5 metres apart. Until the young trees have grown tall, they have to be weeded. As the trees grow, their branches spread outwards. The young forest becomes overcrowded. The weakest trees are cut down to let in more light and air. The stronger trees then have more room to grow.

From time to time the trees are thinned out again. Eventually only the best are left standing. They are still fairly close, though. By being close together they grow upwards, towards the light. And so the trees grow tall and straight.

Fire

The forester's worst enemy is fire. One of the most dangerous times for fires is the early spring. This is when last year's plants have become very dry. Of course, fire is also a danger during hot, dry weather. Some fires are started by lightning. But most are started because someone was careless. Cigarettes, matches and picnic stoves cause many fires.

In all large forest plantations, great care is taken to stop the spread of fire. Between the blocks of trees are large, wide paths. These are known as rides. They help to stop the fire spreading from one block of trees to another. The rides are also useful roads along which felled trees can be taken out of the forest. In some large forests, tall watch towers are built. During the summer a fire-watcher is always on duty in the tower. He or she can spot smoke a long way off and quickly raise the alarm. Near some of the entrances to the forest

A watch tower

there may be fire-beaters. Each of these is a long handle with a rubber flap fixed to it. Anyone seeing a small fire can beat it out with one of these.

Fire can spread quickly through a forest. Trees take many years to grow, but in a few minutes the whole forest can be destroyed.

A forest fire in Australia

Aerial fire-fighting in Canada

18

Do you remember?

1 What is the climate like near the Equator?

2 How do the summers and winters change as you move away from the Equator?

3 What are the three main parts of a tree?

4 How do the roots help a tree?

5 What do leaves need to make food for a tree?

6 What is a deciduous tree?

7 What is an evergreen tree?

8 What happens to the leaves which fall from a tree?

9 Why did the people long ago clear the forests?

10 Name three coniferous trees.

11 Name three deciduous trees.

12 Whereabouts in the world do the big deciduous forests grow?

13 What are the soils like where deciduous forests grow?

14 Why do the plants in a deciduous forest flower early in the spring?

15 Why do the leaves fall from deciduous trees in the autumn?

16 What is the most common kind of deer in northern forests?

17 Name six kinds of things for which trees are used.

18 How is a tree cut so that it falls in the right direction?

19 How have machines made the forester's work easier?

20 How are felled trees usually taken to the sawmills?

21 Why are rivers not used very much nowadays to carry logs to the sawmills?

22 What is coppicing?

23 What is coppiced wood used for?

24 What is a plantation?

25 How may a forester collect tree seeds?

26 Where does a forester sow tree seeds?

27 Why does a forester not sow tree seeds in the forest?

28 Why is a fence put around the land on which young trees are to be planted?

29 Why does a forester plant trees close together?

30 What is a fire-beater like?

Things to do

1 Measure the height of some trees Find a stick which is one metre long. Put that stick in the ground under the tree you wish to measure. Now stand far enough away so that you can see both the stick and the top of the tree.

Hold a pencil at arm's length and move your thumb until the piece of pencil you have uncovered seems to be the same height as your stick. Now see how many times that same piece of pencil goes into the height of the tree.

Suppose the piece of pencil goes into the tree 15 times, that means your tree is roughly 15 metres high.

Use a tape measure or a piece of string and a ruler to measure how far it is round the trunk of the tree. We call this distance the girth of the tree.

Can you find a way to measure how far the branches spread in all directions without climbing the tree?

Which is the tallest tree you can find? How tall is it? Which tree has the biggest girth and the biggest spread of branches? How old do you think each tree is?

2 Measuring the height of tall trees Here is a way of measuring the height of a tall tree. Take a large 45° set-square. Find a place where you can just see the top of the tree while you look along the longest side of the set-square. Keep one of the other sides horizontal as shown in the picture. The height of the tree will be the same as your distance from the tree plus your own height. What is the tallest tree you can find? Many redwood trees in the United States are more than 100 metres high. How much would the tallest tree you can find have to grow to be 100 metres high?

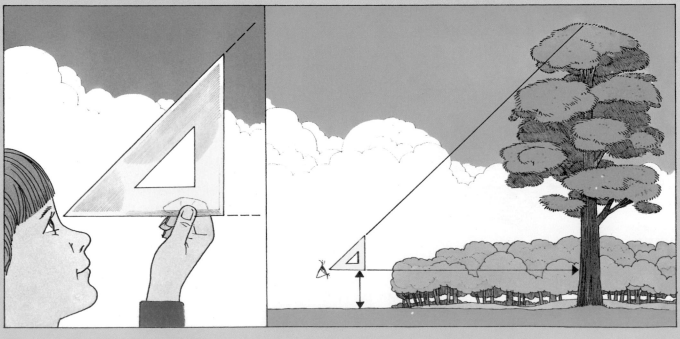

3 Make a collection of bark rubbings

You will need thick drawing paper, drawing pins, and some wax crayons.

Place a sheet of paper against the bark of a tree and fasten it there with the drawing pins. Rub over the paper with a wax crayon until the pattern of the bark shows on the paper. Cut out the pattern and mount it on another piece of paper to make a picture. Write the name of the tree on your bark rubbing.

4 Tree leaves

Collect some tree leaves. Divide your collection into two. In one part put evergreen tree leaves. In the other part put deciduous tree leaves. Look at the leaves carefully. Use a hand lens or magnifying glass to help you to see better. What differences can you see between the two types of leaves, and what similarities?

5 Collecting tree leaves

Make a collection of tree leaves. Take only one or two of the best leaves from each tree.

One way to preserve the leaves is to press them. Arrange the leaves carefully between sheets of newspaper or blotting paper. Press them under bricks or heavy books for several days. Mount the leaves neatly on sheets of card or drawing paper. Label each leaf with the name of the tree.

Another way of making a leaf collection is to make rubbings of them. Lay a leaf flat on the table with the veins uppermost. Place a piece of thin paper over the leaf and make the rubbing as described in number **3** above. Cut out the leaf rubbing and stick it in your book or mount it on card.

6 Preserving leaves in wax

Another way of preserving leaves is to coat them with wax. Ask a grown-up to melt some old candles or paraffin wax (you can buy this at the chemists) for you in an old saucepan. The wax should only just melt, it must **not** boil.

Pick up a leaf by its stalk and quickly lower it into the molten wax. Pull the leaf out again right away. Hold the leaf by the stalk for a few minutes until the wax has set.

Make a display of your waxed leaves. Every leaf should be labelled with the name of the tree it came from.

Try to preserve tree flowers in wax. Can you make a display of these?

Which tree leaves seem to have a natural layer of wax on them?

7 Leafy twigs and water Why do we have to top up the water in vases of flowers from time to time? Where does the water go?

Collect some leafy twigs and some jam-jars. You will also need some olive oil, castor oil, cooking oil or some other vegetable oil, and some sticky labels.

Put one of the leafy twigs in a jar half-filled with water. Mark how far the water comes up the side of the jar with a sticky label, as in the picture.

Take another twig of the same kind and with the same number of leaves. Stand it in a jar half-filled with water. Again mark the water level with a sticky label. Then carefully pour a little vegetable oil on to the water so that it forms a layer 2 or 3 millimetres thick on top of the water.

Have another jam-jar half-filled with water, but with no twig in it. Mark the water level.

Measure the water levels in all three jars every day. Which jar loses the most water? Where does the water go to? Which jar loses the least water? What effect does the oil have? What does the twig do with the water?

Now do the experiment again with only two jars half-filled with water. Put a twig from an evergreen tree in one and a twig from a deciduous tree in the other. Put a layer of oil on the water in both jars. Which jar loses the most water?

8 Where does the water go to which a twig takes up?

Put a leafy twig in a jar half-filled with water. Put a thin layer of vegetable oil on top of the water. Carefully stand the jar and twig in a large polythene bag (one without holes in it), and tie up the top of the bag. What do you see inside the bag after a day or two?

9 Animals in decaying leaves

Study the small animals that live among decaying tree leaves. Spread some sheets of newspaper over the table. Collect a small heap of decaying leaves from a wood or under a hedgerow and put them on the newspaper. Sort through the leaves carefully. Use a magnifying glass to examine any small animals you discover. Count how many of each kind there are. Try and find the names of the animals from books.

You might also try to find a piece of rotting log and examine that. Again try to identify the animals and count them.

Be sure to put everything back under the tree or hedgerow they came from when you have finished your work.

10 How fast do leaves decay?

Which tree leaves decay fastest? You will need some tree leaves of different kinds and some flower pots, yoghurt pots or margarine tubs containing moist garden soil.

Bury one leaf of each kind just under the surface of the soil in each pot. Label the pots with the names of the tree leaves in them. Put the pots on a warm windowsill and keep the soil moist. Every two weeks look at the leaves to see how much has decayed away. Then carefully bury the leaves again. Do some of the leaves decay faster than others?

Put some more leaves in pots of soil. This time use leaves which are all of the same kind. Put some of the pots on a warm

windowsill. Put the others in a cool place – a refrigerator would be ideal. Which leaves decay the fastest? Where would you expect tree leaves to decay the fastest, near the Equator or in the cooler parts of the world?

Try tying small labels on to some dead tree leaves. Tie each leaf to a little stick in the flower border. Look at the leaves every week and see how fast they decay away. Are any of the leaves eaten by animals? Can you find out what kinds of animals eat the leaves? Which kinds of leaves are eaten most?

11 Collecting tree seeds

Collect as many kinds of tree seeds as you can find. Do not forget that conifers produce their seeds in cones. Make sure that any cones are ripe and about to open. You can get the seeds out of a cone by standing the cone near a radiator or in an airing cupboard.

Make a drawing of each seed. Look carefully at its shape, size and colour. Label each drawing carefully. Write against each one the date and place where you found it.

12 Planting tree seeds

Plant some tree fruits and seeds. Good ones to try are acorns, apple pips, beech nuts, sycamore seeds, horse chestnut conkers, elm and ash fruits and pine seeds. You will also need some flower pots, yoghurt pots or margarine containers, and seed compost or a good garden soil.

Plant one tree fruit or seed in each pot of soil or compost. Bury the seeds about 5 millimetres deep. Put the pots on a warm windowsill and keep the soil or compost moist. Be patient, since some tree seeds are very slow to grow.

Record carefully what happens to the seeds in each of your pots. Make drawings to show what the seedlings look like. Measure the seedlings regularly and make graphs to show how they grow.

Plant some seeds upside down and some on their sides. Do they grow?

Keep some pots containing seeds planted the right way up in a warm room and some out of doors in the cold. Keep some more pots in the light and some in the dark. Make sure the soil in all the pots stays moist. Make notes or drawings to show what happens in each experiment. What have you learned about growing tree seeds?

13 Friends and enemies of the forester

Find out all you can about the animals and plants which are friends and enemies of the forester. Make a book about them.

14 Temperate forest fruits

Make a collection of the labels from cartons and cans of fruits grown in the temperate parts of the world. Stick your labels on a large sheet of card. Against each label write down the name of the country in which the fruits were grown.

15 Write a story

Write a story called 'A year in the life of a fruit farmer.'

16 A tree diary or scrapbook

Keep a diary or scrapbook about one tree which is near to your home or school. Study the tree for a whole year. What kind of tree is it?

Make drawings or paintings, or take photographs, to show your tree in summer and winter. Write down as many measurements as you can for your tree: its height, girth and how far its branches spread, for example. Collect bark rubbings, twigs, and leaves or leaf prints. Press a few of the tree's flowers and mount examples of its fruits or seeds.

What is the timber of the tree used for? Can you obtain a small piece of that kind of timber for your book? A carpenter might be able to give you a piece.

Make lists or drawings of any birds, insects or other small animals you see on your tree. Write notes about their life histories.

Things to find out

1 Look at a map of the world which shows the distribution of temperate forests. Roughly what is the greatest distance temperate forests occur north or south of the polar regions?

2 Collect as many kinds of fallen leaves as you can. Try to find out their names.

3 A few conifers are also deciduous. Find out which trees these are and where they like to grow.

4 Find out about the different ways in which trees spread their fruits and seeds to new areas.

5 Why are the temperatures near the Equator higher than those towards the polar regions? Why are the days all about the same length throughout the year? Why is it colder nearer the polar regions?

6 How do trees and other plants affect the air? Why are trees often planted by the sides of roads in towns?

7 Mineral salts are vital to the growth of plants. In a forest there are many mineral salts in the trees. What happens to these mineral salts if the tree is cut down and used as firewood in someone's home?

When farmers send crops to market, what happens to the mineral salts in the plants? How do farmers put mineral salts back into the soil to make up for those which have been lost? Do foresters ever do this? If so, how?

8 Hedges and shelter-belts are really long thin forests. Why were hedges and shelter-belts planted? How long ago were they planted? Why are hedges often dug up or burned down nowadays?

9 Why is it that two forests the same distance from the Equator may have completely different climates?

10 In the 16th century to build a large ship took nearly 2000 large trees. Find out what kinds of trees were used for ship-building and how the ships were built.

11 Study your atlas. How many continents can you find which contain a large area of temperate forest? Name a country in each of these continents which contains a large temperate forest. Is the forest deciduous or coniferous?

25

Wood

Bark being removed from logs in Finland

Wood or timber is the natural material we obtain from trees. After a tree has been cut down the branches and bark are removed. The trunk is then cut into thick planks.

Logs and planks being seasoned

Before the wood can be used it has to be dried slowly and carefully. This is called seasoning. If the wood is not seasoned it may later twist or bend. Sometimes the wood is dried in the

open air. More often it is dried in a special oven called a kiln. Warm air is blown between the planks.

Sawn trunks

Not all wood is seasoned. A lot of wood is chopped up into smaller pieces and made into pulp. From this pulp, many everyday things can be made. Nothing is wasted at the sawmill. The bark is used to fire the kilns that season the wood. Any sawdust goes to make wood pulp or chipboard.

Logs are 'shaved' to make thin veneers

Other kinds of wood

Veneering a table

Not all kinds of wood are as simple as they seem. Sometimes logs of expensive kinds of wood are peeled into very thin sheets. A thin layer of this expensive wood is stuck onto a cheaper wood. This thin layer of wood is called a veneer. Usually the veneer has an attractive pattern, or grain, on it. A lot of furniture is made from veneered wood.

Veneered furniture

Plywood is made by sticking together thin sheets of wood. If you look at the edges of a piece of plywood you can see how many layers of wood were used to make it. Blockboard is made from lengths of wood stuck together. These strips of wood are glued between two thin sheets of wood like a sandwich. Blockboard makes a very strong plank.

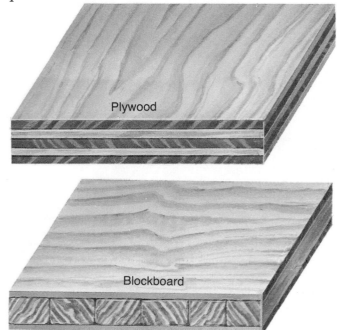

Chipboard is also a timber made by people. Wood is chopped up into tiny pieces, or chips. These chips are mixed with glue and pressed into large boards. A lot of chipboard is used to make furniture, but first it is covered with a veneer.

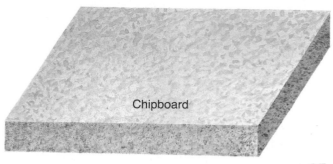

Paper

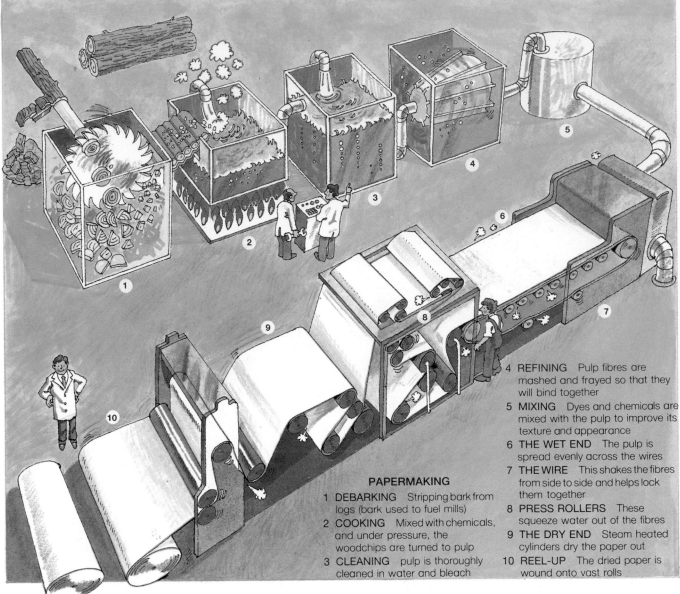

PAPERMAKING

1 DEBARKING Stripping bark from logs (bark used to fuel mills)

2 COOKING Mixed with chemicals, and under pressure, the woodchips are turned to pulp

3 CLEANING pulp is thoroughly cleaned in water and bleach

4 REFINING Pulp fibres are mashed and frayed so that they will bind together

5 MIXING Dyes and chemicals are mixed with the pulp to improve its texture and appearance

6 THE WET END The pulp is spread evenly across the wires

7 THE WIRE This shakes the fibres from side to side and helps lock them together

8 PRESS ROLLERS These squeeze water out of the fibres

9 THE DRY END Steam heated cylinders dry the paper out

10 REEL-UP The dried paper is wound onto vast rolls

Some paper is made from waste paper. But most is made from wood. The logs are first chopped up into small chips. These wood chips are then boiled with a chemical called caustic soda. This turns the wood chips into a soft pulpy mass. The wood pulp looks a little like papier mâché. The pulp is bleached to make it white. It is then drained on to a fine wire sieve before it goes into the paper machine.

In the paper machine there is a large conveyor belt. The pulp is spread over the belt as it moves along. The water is removed from the pulp. Then the pulp is passed between large rollers. These press it out into a thin sheet. The paper is finished by passing it through heated rollers to make it smooth.

Paper is used for writing and printing and making books like this one. It is also used for tissues, tickets, bank notes and posters. It is even used for some kinds of clothing.

Charcoal

Charcoal is partly burnt wood. It is used mainly for cooking and sometimes for heating. Some charcoal is used in making certain metals. It is also used for drawing and in making inks, paints, rubber, gunpowder and fireworks.

Drawing with charcoal

A charcoal kiln

Charcoal is usually produced in a kiln. The kiln is made of metal or soil. Short pieces of wood are packed into the kiln. A space is left down the centre to act as a chimney. Air-holes are made around the sides. Then the kiln is closed. A fire is started in the kiln through one of the air-holes. The fire is left to burn for a day or so until the smoke coming from it is no longer black. When the smoke has turned to a blue colour, the chimney and all the air-holes are closed. The fire is then left for two or three days more until the fire dies down.

When the kiln is cool, it is opened. The black charcoal is removed. Making charcoal uses pieces of wood that would otherwise be wasted. All the branches of a tree can be used except the smallest ones.

Cross-section of a charcoal kiln

Apple orchards

Wild crab apples in a hedgerow

About 30 kinds of apple trees grow wild in the temperate forests. But hundreds of different kinds of new apple trees have been bred from these by scientists. Most apple trees are grown in orchards. Usually they are planted on slopes facing the sun. This makes it warmer during the day and helps the fruit to ripen. Trees are not planted in the bottom of valleys where cold air will collect. Often hedges or rows of tall trees are planted around the orchards to protect them from damage by the wind.

Apple orchard in spring

Picking the apple crop

Nowadays apple trees are kept smaller so that the fruit is easy to pick. The trees are shaped by pruning. This is done during the winter when the trees have stopped growing. During the spring the apple trees blossom. Bee hives are brought into the orchard. The bees can then carry pollen from one apple flower to another. After this, young apples grow from the flowers.

In the autumn the apples are picked. They are sorted and packed into large wooden boxes. Only the best apples are packed. They are stored in very cold buildings. This keeps the apples fresh. And so we can have fresh apples at any time of the year. When they are needed, the apples are packed in cardboard boxes and taken to the shops and markets.

Grading apples for size and quality

The hunting forests of Europe

Thousands of years ago people had to hunt. They killed animals for their meat or to make clothing and tools. Later, as we have seen, many of the deciduous forests were cleared to make way for crops. Hunting still went on though. It was the only way to get fresh meat in winter. This was because there was never enough food to keep the farm animals alive in winter. Most of them were killed in the autumn and the meat was preserved with salt or smoke. But people also hunted for fun.

As more fields were made, there were fewer forests to hunt in. In the Middle Ages (1066–1485), the lords began to take over forests. King William the Conqueror claimed large areas of forest in England as hunting grounds. The same kind of thing happened in France, Germany, Spain and other parts of Europe. In these forests only kings or lords were allowed to hunt. Anyone else who hunted the deer, wild boar or other animals was severely punished.

After the Middle Ages hunting continued. Because of the hunting, forests were saved which would otherwise have been cleared for fields. Many of the deciduous forests which remain today are there because of hunting now or in the past.

Nowadays there are still whole areas of forest in France and Britain where people are banned. This is so that the animals can live and breed in peace, and so that there will always be wild animals to hunt.

The forests of the Mediterranean region

Long ago dense evergreen forests covered most of the land around the Mediterranean Sea. These forests were mainly of pines and evergreen oaks. From one kind of evergreen oak, cork was obtained. These evergreen trees grew well in the hot dry summers and mild wet winters around the Mediterranean.

Taking cork bark from the cork oak

Olive groves in Spain

But most of the trees were cut down. Their trunks and branches were used for timber and firewood. The leaves and twigs were fed to goats and other farm animals. Large areas of the forest were also cleared to make fields. There were many fires, some accidental, some deliberate. Sheep and goats ate any young trees which grew in the bare ground. In many places, with no covering of plants, the fertile soil was blown or washed away. Where this happened, some of the once fertile land became a desert area.

Only a little of the original forest remains today. There are however patches of scrub in some places. There are also groups of olive trees. People brought these to the Mediterranean area long ago for their fruits and the oil made from them. Nowadays, however, most olive trees are grown in special orchards or groves.

Some of the remaining pine forest in the Mediterranean

The northern coniferous forests

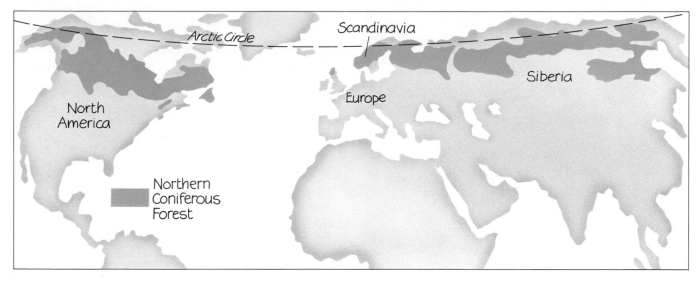

A huge belt of coniferous forest stretches right across the Earth. In places it is 2000 kilometres wide. The forest stretches across Scandinavia, northern Europe, Siberia and the whole of North America.

Walking in a Scandinavian forest

In these areas the climate is often difficult. The winters are long and cold, with heavy falls of snow. The summers are short and cool. During the short summer the sun hardly sets below the horizon.

The trees in all these northern forests are similar. Although birch trees grow here and there, most of the trees are conifers. Pine, spruce and fir trees grow in huge patches. The densely-packed trees grow tall and straight. Little light reaches the ground. Because of this, few other plants grow beneath the trees. Most of these coniferous forests have never been cleared to make fields. This is because the soils are poor. Most crops would not grow because of the short summers.

Wood anemones like to grow in forest shade

People in the northern coniferous forests

Lumberman at work on a spruce

Logs floating down to sawmills in Canada

Few people live in the northern coniferous forests. As we have seen, the soil is too poor and the summers too short for there to be farms. Some people earn a living by hunting and trapping animals. The animals are used for their fur. Other people are lumbermen. Their job is to fell trees. Many of the lumbermen are farm workers from further south. They work in the forests during the winter when there is no work on the farms.

Since the different kinds of trees grow in large patches, it is easy for the lumbermen to fell trees of all one kind. Some of the logs are floated down rivers to the sawmills. Others are moved by lorry or train. At the sawmills the large logs are made into planks. The smaller logs are crushed into pulp for making paper or cardboard.

Gold, silver, copper, iron, nickel and uranium are valuable minerals found in the northern forest areas. Oil and coal are also found there. Some

of the largest towns and villages have grown up where these minerals are mined. Because it is not possible to farm the land, all of the food for the miners and lumbermen has to be brought in by aircraft.

Hunting deer with a muzzle-loading rifle

34

The tallest and oldest trees in the world

The tallest trees in the world are the redwoods. These giant trees grow along the Pacific coast of North America. They grow in the fertile soils where the rivers flow down from the mountains. Many of the older redwood trees are over 100 metres high. They are as much as 12 metres in circumference. Some are more than 3000 years old.

Giant redwood trees in California, USA

The redwoods grow so well because each year the rivers flood. The floodwaters drop fertile mud around the trees. The redwoods grow new roots in this layer of mud. Other trees round about cannot do this, and die. The redwoods can then grow unhindered.

The oldest trees in the world are also conifers. They grow inland from the redwood forests. These old trees are called bristlecone pines. They grow on the dry, stony slopes of the Rocky Mountains. They are rarely more than 10 metres high. But the oldest is 4600 years old. Most of the redwoods and bristlecone pines were cut down by people to use for buildings and railway sleepers. Now those which remain grow protected in nature reserves and national parks.

Bristlecone pine trees

China and Japan

Both China and Japan once had large natural forests. But most of these were cleared long ago. In Japan, however, new forests were soon planted. Rough mountain land was planted with forests. This land was not suitable for farming. The forests are growing faster than the trees are being felled. Now two-thirds of Japan is covered with these forests. And a big timber industry is being built up.

In China, however, the forests were not replanted right away. Floods have often caused great damage and loss of life in China. Crops have been destroyed. Fertile soil has been washed away. All these things happened because there were no forests to take up some of the heavy rain. Until recently in China, firewood and building timber were scarce. It was even difficult to find timber for coffins. Now large new forests are being planted. But it will be many years before China has enough timber.

Japanese forest and lakeland

Australian eucalyptus forests

Budgerigars in their natural habitat

A koala in a eucalyptus tree

Australia has a smaller part of its area in forest than any other continent. This is because much of Australia is desert or semi-desert. Most of the forests are in the coastal areas. Some are tropical forests, but about half are temperate forests.

The most important trees in Australia belong to the eucalyptus family. Eucalyptus trees have flat crowns. Their leaves have a waxy coating to cut down the loss of water. The trees grow to enormous sizes. The Karri tree sometimes reaches 100 metres high. Its timber is used in mines and for making docks and harbours. It is also used a great deal in houses for furniture, panelling and flooring. Honey of the best kind comes from bees which have fed on the flowers of the Karri tree. The Jarrah tree is another kind of eucalyptus tree.

The Australian forests are the home of the grey kangaroo. Flocks of green budgerigars fly through the trees. Wombats, opossums and koalas live in and beneath the trees. There are also some kinds of pine trees in these temperate parts of Australia. However, many more pine trees are grown in plantations. A lot of these pines have been brought from other countries.

An inquisitive tree opossum

Forests for leisure

Forests are good places for people to walk in the peace and fresh air. It is particularly easy to walk in forest plantations where there are large rides or paths.

In many forests there are places to camp or caravan. There are picnic sites. Footpaths have been signposted. Nature trails have been laid out. As the people walk along these marked paths, they can study the plants and animals with the help of a guide book or notice boards. Special shelters, or hides, have been put up from where people can watch the birds, deer and other animals. Some forests have trails for pony trekking.

In winter some of the northern forests are used for skiing. In other forests hunting is allowed. Fishing and boating take place in the forest lakes and rivers. However, a few visitors are a nuisance. Sometimes they leave litter or damage trees. Even more dangerous is the risk that visitors to the forests may start a fire.

Camping, and (inset) trekking in the forest

The forests return

Forest clearance in Canada

As we have seen in this book, many of the world's forests have been cut down. The forests have been cut down for their timber and to make paper. They have been cut down to make farms where food can be produced. The forests have also been cleared to make room for roads, houses, shops, factories, mines and other buildings.

People have planted some new forests. These are largely of quick-growing conifers. However, given time, forests like the original ones could return. In 1882 a wheat field in England was left untouched. Wild grasses quickly covered the field. Gradually other plants appeared. Eventually these were replaced by shrubs and small trees. Now the field is covered by oak woodland. It is called the Broadbalk Wilderness. This woodland is identical to other natural woodland growing in the area.

Forest would return to many of the places from which it was cleared if it was given the chance. In the north-eastern United States, a lot of people abandoned their farms in the 1850s. Now large trees grow among the crumbling buildings and deserted fields. These new forests are similar to the ones which the American settlers cleared to make their fields. The tree seeds were carried there by birds, animals and the wind. Even a town garden would turn to woodland if it was left long enough.

The Broadbalk Wilderness

A ruined farmstead

Do you remember?

1 After a tree has been cut down, what is done to the bark and branches?

2 Why is wood seasoned?

3 How is wood seasoned?

4 What is a veneer?

5 How is plywood made?

6 How is blockboard made?

7 How is chipboard made?

8 What is most paper made from?

9 What is charcoal?

10 What is charcoal used for?

11 Where are most apple trees grown?

12 Why are most apple trees kept small nowadays?

13 Why are bee hives brought into orchards in the spring?

14 Why did people have to hunt in the past, particularly in winter?

15 What were the two main kinds of evergreen trees in the forests around the Mediterranean?

16 Why were the forests around the Mediterranean cut down?

17 Name three countries in which the northern coniferous forests occur.

18 What are the winters like in the northern coniferous forests?

19 Why have most of the northern coniferous forests never been cleared?

20 What is the work of a lumberman?

21 What are the tallest trees in the world?

22 What are the oldest trees in the world?

23 What has been done in Japan to replace the large natural forests?

24 What happened in China when the forests were not replanted?

25 What are the most important trees in the Australian forests?

26 Name three wild animals which live in the Australian forests.

27 In what ways are forests used for leisure activities?

28 What is a nature trail?

29 Give four reasons why the world's forests have been cut down.

30 What happened to the wheat field in England which was left untouched?

Things to do

1 Things made of wood
Make a list of things which are made partly or completely of wood. Look around your home or school for ideas. Think carefully about each of the things on your list. Are there any materials which could be used instead of wood in the things on your list? Write these down as well.

2 Experiments with timber
Collect some small blocks or off-cuts of different kinds of timber. You might be able to obtain some of these off-cuts from a carpenter.

Look at the different kinds of timber with a hand lens or magnifying glass. Look at the different patterns or grain on them. Wet each of the blocks of wood with water. How does the appearance of each block of wood change?

Try floating the blocks of wood in a bowl of water. Which kinds float the best? Do any kinds of timber sink?

Weigh some of the blocks of wood before you float them. Leave them in the water for a day or two. Then wipe them dry and weigh them again. Which kinds of timber have taken up the most water?

Carefully knock a nail into each of the blocks of wood. Which block of wood does a nail go into easiest and which is the hardest to knock a nail into? Which timber is the easiest to scratch with a nail and which is the hardest?

Mix some poster paint and paint your blocks of timber. Which kind is the easiest to paint and which is the hardest? Why are some of the blocks of wood hard to paint?

If you had plenty of each kind of timber, which would make the best workbench? Which timber would make the best boat? Which timber would it be easiest to use for wood carving? Why would you choose each kind of timber?

3 Make a collection of timbers
Make a collection of small pieces of the timbers that come from deciduous and evergreen trees. Label your collection. Try to find out what each of these timbers is used for.

4 Knots in wood
The side branches of a tree make small rings and ovals in the wood when it is cut into planks. Often these knots have beautiful waves in them, and wood with knots in it is used in some fine furniture. Draw some knots in wood carefully and colour them. Sometimes plastic is painted to imitate the pattern of knots in wood and it is then used as a veneer on furniture.

5 A collection of different kinds of paper Make a collection of different kinds of paper. Try to include newspaper, greaseproof paper, blotting paper, typing paper and as many other kinds of paper as you can. Display your collection in your classroom.

shape you want. The heads of people (or puppets) and animals, and simple shapes like owls, are easy to make. Leave the shape to dry in a warm room. In a few days it will dry and harden, like the wood it came from originally. Paint your papier mâché shapes.

6 Papier mâché Make some papier mâché. Tear up old newspapers or tissues into small pieces – the smaller the pieces the better. Get a bowl of water and add a little wallpaper paste to the water and stir it in. If you do not have any wallpaper paste, you can use flour-and-water paste. Soak the pieces of paper in the liquid, stirring them from time to time.

When you get a good pulpy mass, squeeze the water out of it. It looks very much like the wood pulp from which paper is made. Mould the papier mâché into the

7 Waste paper As we read earlier, paper is made from trees. But as we have also read, many of the world's forests are being cut down. Paper can also be made from old waste paper. For every 1 tonne of waste paper used again in this way, 17 trees are saved.

Ask your teacher if you can organise a waste paper collection in your school. The paper could be used to raise money for a charity or for your school funds. Not only will you be raising money for a good cause, you will also be saving our precious forests.

Glossary

Here are the meanings of some words which you might have met for the first time in this book.

Carbon dioxide: a gas in the air which is used by green plants to make their food.

Charcoal: a black or dark grey substance made from partly burned wood.

Chlorophyll: the green substance which gives plants their colouring, and with which they trap sunlight to help make their food.

Conifers: trees which do not have proper flowers although they do have separate male and female parts. The female part develops into a cone which contains seeds. Most conifers have needle-shaped leaves like those of pine or spruce trees.

Coniferous forest: a forest of conifer trees.

Coppicing: the cutting back of certain small trees from time to time so that they produce large quantities of thin sticks when they make fresh growth.

Crown: the name given to the part of a tree above the trunk. The crown is made up of branches, twigs and leaves.

Decay: to rot away.

Deciduous tree: a tree which loses its leaves in the autumn and grows new ones the following spring.

Equator: the imaginary line passing round the middle of the Earth.

Evergreen tree: a tree which does not lose all its leaves in the autumn, but instead, loses them a few at a time throughout the year.

Fertile: a good soil which is capable of growing many crops is said to be fertile.

Fuel: anything which will burn and produce heat.

Kiln: a large oven in which wood is seasoned or in which charcoal is made.

Lumberman: a man whose work is to fell trees.

Mineral salts: the chemical substances which trees and other plants obtain from the soil and use as food.

National park: a large area of land over which special care is taken to see that the beautiful scenery is not spoilt and where the plants and animals are protected.

Orchards: a plantation in which fruit trees are grown.

Plantations: forests which have been planted by people.

Polar regions: the regions with short summers and long cold winters around the North and South Poles.

Poles: North and South Poles. The ends of the Earth's imaginary axis on which it spins.

Pruning: the cutting away of branches from trees or bushes to stop them growing too tall, to change their shape, or to make them bear more flowers or fruit.

Seasoning: the slow and careful drying of wood before it can be used. If wood is not seasoned it may later twist, warp or bend.

Temperate regions: the parts of the world between the tropics and the polar regions. The temperate regions have all kinds of weather.

Timber: the name given to the wood of a tree.

Tree-line: the imaginary line on a mountain above which it is too cold or too windy for trees to grow.

Tropics: the zone of the Earth on either side of the Equator where the sun is directly overhead all through the year and where there is little difference between the seasons.

Trunk: the large, woody stem of a tree.

Veneer: a thin layer of expensive wood which is stuck on to cheaper wood.

Index

A
air 6, 17, 26, 30, 38
animals 7, 11, 12, 16, 17, 23, 31, 32, 34, 38, 39, 44
annual rings 43, 44
apple 13, 24, 30, 46
ash 6, 10, 24
Australia 18, 26, 37
autumn 11, 12, 17, 30, 31
axe 14

B
bacteria 7
bark 21, 26, 32
bark rubbing 21, 24
bears 8, 11, 12
beech 6, 24
bees 30, 37
birch 10, 33
birds 16, 38, 39
bison 8, 12
blockboard 27
bluebells 11
branches 5, 7, 9, 10, 11, 14, 17, 20, 24, 26, 29, 32
bristlecone pines 35
Britain 31
Broadbalk Wilderness 39
buds 5, 11
buildings 13, 30, 35, 39

C
California 35
Cambridgeshire 16
Canada 9, 15
carbon dioxide 6
cardboard 34
carpenter 24, 41
caterpillars 10
caustic soda 28
chainsaw 14
charcoal 13, 29
China 36, 46
chipboard 26, 27
chipmunks 11
chips 14, 27, 28
chlorophyll 6
clearings 8, 12
climate 4, 33
cones 9, 23
coniferous forests 10, 33, 34
conifers 9, 10, 23, 33, 35, 37
coppicing 16
cork 13, 32
crab apples 30
crops 8, 31, 33, 36
crown 5

D
damage 30, 36
danger 18
decay 7, 23
deciduous trees 6, 8, 9, 10, 11, 16, 22, 31
deer 8, 11, 12, 31, 38
desert 32, 37
dormouse 11

E
earthworms 7
elm 6, 10
England 31, 39
Equator 4, 10, 23

eucalyptus 37
Europe 8, 10, 12, 31, 32
evergreen oak 32
evergreen trees 6, 7, 8, 9. 11, 21, 22, 32, 41

F
farmland 10
felling 14
fertile soil 10, 32, 35, 36
fertilizers 7
fields 31–33, 39
fir 8, 9, 33
fire 8, 18, 29, 38, 44
fire-beater 18, 19
firewood 16, 32, 36
floods 35, 36
flowers 5, 30, 37
food 6, 7, 8, 11, 31, 34, 39, 44
forester 16, 18, 24
France 13, 31
fruit 11, 24, 30, 32
fuel 13
fungi 7, 11
furniture 13, 27, 37, 41
furniture beetle 46

G
Germany 31
girth 20, 24
glue 27
grain 27, 41
growth 25, 44

H
hardwoods 46
hedgehog 11
hedges 25, 30
height 20, 24
herds 8, 12
hibernation 11
hides 38
holly 6, 7
honey 37
houses 13, 37
hunting 31, 34, 38

I
insects 10, 11

J
Japan 36
Jarrah tree 37

K
kangaroo 37
Karri tree 37
kiln 26, 29
knots 41
koalas 37

L
lakes 38
land 17, 32, 36
landowners 46
laurel 6
leaf rubbing 21
leaves 5–7, 9–12, 21–23 32, 37
leisure 38
light 11, 17, 24, 33
lightning 18
litter 38
logs 14, 15, 26–28, 34, 44
lumberman 34
lynx 8, 12

M
machines 14
measuring 20
Mediterranean 32

Middle Ages 31
millipedes 7
minerals 34
mineral salts 6, 7, 25
miniature forest 45
mining 34, 37, 39
mountain 9, 35, 36

N
national forest 16
national park 35
natural regeneration 44
nature trails 38
newspaper 28, 42
New Zealand 12
North America 8, 10, 12, 33, 35
North Pole 4

O
oak 5–7, 10, 32, 39
oil 34
olive 32
opossum 37
orchards 30, 32
oxygen 6

P
Pacific coast 35
paper 13, 14, 28, 34, 39, 42
papier mâché 28, 42
paths 18, 38
peace 31, 38
people 8, 10, 12, 13, 16, 17, 31, 32, 34, 35, 39
pines 6, 8, 9, 24, 32, 33, 37
plank 26, 27, 34, 41
plantations 13, 14, 16–18, 37, 38
plants 7, 8, 11, 18, 32, 33
plywood 27
polar regions 4, 9, 25
pollen 30
preserving leaves 21, 22
pruning 30
pulp mills 15

R
rain 4, 7, 36
rayon 13, 46
redwood trees 20, 35
river 15, 34, 35, 38
road 8, 15, 18, 39
Rocky Mountains 35
roots 5, 6, 35
rotting 7

S
sawmill 15, 26, 34
saws 14
Scandinavia 33
seasoning 26
seasons 4, 11
seedlings 16, 45
seeds 8, 9, 11, 16, 23, 24, 39, 44
semi-desert 37
settlers 12, 39
shelter-belts 25
ship-building 25
Siberia 33
smoke 18, 29, 31
snow 9, 33
softwoods 46
soil 5–7, 9, 11, 23, 24, 29, 33, 34
South Pole 4
Spain 31, 32
spring 6, 11, 17, 18, 30

spruce 8, 9, 33
stem 5
Stone Age 13
summer 4, 6, 10, 12, 24, 32–34, 43
sun 6, 10, 30, 33
sycamore 6, 10, 24

T
tap root 5
temperate regions 4, 9, 46
temperatures 11, 25
timber 14, 15, 24, 26, 27, 32, 36, 37, 39, 41
trapping 34
tree bicycle 16
tree diary 24
tree-hugger 14
tree-line 9
tree nursery 16
tropics 4
trunk 5, 7, 14–16, 20, 26, 32, 43
twig 5, 7, 22, 23, 32

U
United States of America 20, 39, 46

V
veins 6
veneer 27, 41

W
wapiti 12
waste-paper 28, 42
water 5, 6, 9, 11, 22, 23, 28, 37, 41, 42
weather 4, 11, 18, 43
wheat field 39
wild boar 31
wind 5, 7, 30, 39
winter 4, 7, 9–11, 15, 17, 24, 30–34
wolves 8, 12
wombats 37
wood 13, 26–29, 41
wood anemones 33
woodland 7, 17, 39, 44
wood lice 7
wood pulp 13, 26, 28, 42, 46
woodworm 46

Y
yew 6

14 Grow a miniature forest

If you have grown a number of seedling trees you could make a miniature forest for your classroom.

Obtain a large shallow box or a large seed tray. You will also need some peat or seed compost. Arrange your pots of trees in the box or seed tray. Then cover the pots with peat or compost, making small hills in places. You could make paths between the trees with moss. As long as you keep it cut short with scissors, you could sow grass seed between the trees. Do not forget to keep the peat or compost moist. Perhaps you could make a model log cabin from twigs to stand in your forest. A painted cardboard background will complete your miniature forest.

Things to find out

1 Draw or trace an outline map of the world. Shade in the areas where large temperate forests occur. Mark in any large rivers which flow through these forests. Find out more about these rivers.

2 Find out all you can about conifer plantations. What kinds of trees grow there? Why are they so tall? For what purposes is the timber used? Why are pines and other conifers grown instead of deciduous trees?

3 A lot of apple and other fruit trees are no longer grown from seeds. Find out how new trees are grown and why this method is often preferred.

4 Fire is the forester's biggest enemy in most countries. But in the United States, certain conifers need fire before they will grow. Find out about these conifers and how fire helps them.

5 Foresters and carpenters often talk about 'hardwoods' and 'softwoods'. What do they mean by these terms? What kinds of trees do hardwoods and softwoods come from?

6 Rayon is made from wood pulp. Find out more about how rayon is made and what it is used for.

7 During the 18th century, rich landowners in many parts of the world began planting trees to decorate their parks. Find out more about the trees they planted. Which countries did the trees come from? Which is the nearest of these parks to your home or school?

8 One of the big enemies of timber in buildings and furniture is the woodworm.

The woodworm is not really a worm but a beetle, sometimes called the furniture beetle. Find out all you can about woodworms or furniture beetles. Where do they live? What do they feed on? What damage do they cause? How are they got rid of?

A woodworm grub can ruin woodwork

9 Find out about the animals which were hunted in forests during the Middle Ages. What methods were used to catch the anima

10 Choose an animal which lives in one of the temperate forests. Find out all you can about it. How is it able to survive in the forest? What enemies does it have? Collect as many pictures as you can of your chosen animal. Make a book about your animal.

11 In China, the rivers flooded more often after the forests around them had been cut down. Find out what effect a forest has on a river running through it. Why is the river more likely to flood if the trees are removed?

12 Rotting or decay is a natural process in a forest. But it can be a great nuisance if wooden furniture or buildings begin to rot. What is done to wood to stop it rotting?

8 Annual rings

If the trunk of a tree is cut across, we can see rings in the wood. These are called annual rings. A tree grows one of these rings every year. So by counting the rings, we can tell the age of a tree. If the weather is cold or dry one summer, the trunk will not grow so much, and the ring produced that year will be narrow. If the weather is warm and wet, the trunk will grow a lot, and that year's ring will be wider.

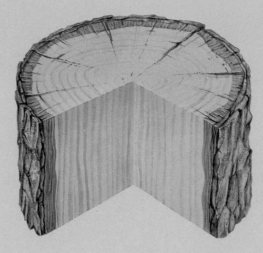

This tree is 134 years old

A 1851 The Great Exhibition, Crystal Palace
B 1869 Suez Canal opened
C 1880 Edison invents the electric light
D 1896 'The Daily Mail' newspaper begins
E 1900 Death of Queen Victoria
F 1914 First World War begins
G 1926 J.L.Baird invents television
H 1936 King Edward VIII abdicates
I 1940 The Battle of Britain
J 1953 Edmund Hillary climbs Mount Everest
K 1969 Neil Armstrong is first man on moon
L 1973 Britain joins the E.E.C.
M 1980 Olympic Games held in Moscow

You can study the age and growth of a tree if you obtain a large log or a section of a really old tree. If you cannot obtain either of these, try to find a large tree stump. Sandpaper the cut surface of the stump until it is clean and smooth and the rings show up.

The ring on the outside of the log or tree stump will be the year in which the tree was felled. Find out what year that was.

When you know the date of the outside ring, count each ring into the centre. How many are there? In which year did the tree begin its life?

Find out some things which happened during the tree's life. Here are some things you could find out:

When such things as radios, telephones, televisions and cameras were invented.

Which kings, queens, presidents or prime ministers were in power.

Which wars were fought.

What famous events took place.

When you and the members of your family were born.

Make little flags fixed to pins. Stick them in the annual ring for the year in which these things happened.

9 Forest fires Paint a picture of a forest fire. Then write a story about your picture and the fire it shows.

10 A time machine Pretend you have a time machine which will allow you to go back into the past. Pretend that you go back thousands of years to the time when much of the land was covered by forests. Write a story about a day in your life. What is the countryside around you like? What wild animals are there? What do you eat? How do you collect or catch your food? How do you keep yourself warm? Remember that many of the materials we use today would not have been available then.

11 A collection of nuts Make a collection of different kinds of nuts. If you want to make the shells shiny, paint them with clear vanish. Glue the nuts on to a sheet of card. Label each one with its name and where it was probably grown.

12 Collect pictures of forest animals Collect pictures of animals which live in woodlands and forests. Sort your pictures into those of animals which live in deciduous forests and those which live in coniferous forests. Can you find any animals which live in both kinds of forest?

Make wallcharts with your pictures. Write something about each of your pictures.

13 Natural regeneration As we have seen, some tree seeds do grow in woods and forests. That is how the forest continues to grow when the old trees die. This is known as natural regeneration. If you go into a wood or forest, see how many young trees you can find growing near an old tree. Are they the same as the old tree? Count the young trees. How many of them do you think will grow to be large trees?